SUNBURST HERITAGE SERIES

HISTORIC HOUSES
OF BRITAIN

SUNBURST HERITAGE SERIES

HISTORIC HOUSES OF BRITAIN

GARRY GIBBONS

SUNBURST BOOKS

For Ria and Merry

The publishers wish to dedicate this title and the others in the series to Don Webb,
to mark his contribution to book buying

This edition first published 1994 by Sunburst Books, an imprint of the Promotional Reprint
Company Limited, Deacon House, 65 Old Church Street, London SW3 5BS

Designed by Anthony Cohen
Printed and bound in China

ISBN 1 85778 049 3

Cover photograph: Buckingham Palace, London
Half title photograph: Dunrobin Castle, Highlands
Title page photograph: Longleat House, Wiltshire

CONTENTS

Introduction 6

ENGLAND

WALES

SCOTLAND

Map of England, Scotland and Wales 96

INTRODUCTION

The victory of Henry Tudor over Richard III at Bosworth in 1485 brought an end to the Wars of the Roses and thereby settled the rivalry which had existed for over thirty years between the royal houses of York and Lancaster. The powerful feudal lords and their private armies gave way to a strong central government.

The peaceful era of Tudor rule meant that the ancient feudal castles had outlived their usefulness and they started to fall into disrepair. Many were adapted from their original defensive role by the addition of large windows, even on the ground floor. Further extensions to the domestic quarters ensured that these old family strongholds would continue to be inhabited for many centuries. The great Tudor houses which began to appear towards the end of the 15th century replaced the outdated fortified home. Wide latticed windows, protruding oriel windows and light, spacious rooms gave the mansions an outward-looking appearance. Echoes of past fortifications were displayed in the retention of crenellations and, occasionally, gate houses, but these were purely stylistic.

Many of England's great families date from this time, including the Cecils, the Herberts, the Russells and the Thynnes. These families were headed by ambitious men who were to form the newly emerging class of powerful administrators.

Their stature was reflected in the size of the palaces which they built. These constructions were capable of housing royal visitors accompanied by a large retinue.

The most popular plan of these early mansions continued to be based on the old fortified design, comprising an inner courtyard surrounded by ranges of rooms, one room in depth, one leading into the other, with the entrance to the courtyard by way of a gate house. The proliferation of ornate chimneys bore testimony to the increased comfort within. Gradually, the gate house and inner courtyard disappeared, along with the two remaining wings, leaving a single rectangular building which was to expand vertically through two or more storeys.

The largest of the early palaces was Hampton Court (see inset, page 34). Built by Cardinal Wolsey between 1515 and 1530, Hampton marked the beginning of the English Renaissance. Although the style is obviously Tudor, indicated by the red brick and the retention of medieval Gothic features, the decorations were Italian, and included busts and medallions of Roman emperors in terracotta. Almost as wealthy as the King himself, the Cardinal was a great prince of the Roman church and lived accordingly. He drew on vast revenues to maintain his household, which was almost a thousand strong, and marched in state preceded by ornamental silver pillars and deadly pole-axes. Standards of living rose slowly throughout the Tudor period, and not only among the upper classes. An unknown writer of 1577 records,

> "Our Fathers, yea and we ourselves have lien full oft upon straw pallets, covered only with a sheet, under coverlets made of dagswain or hop harlots and a good round log under their heads instead of a bolster. If it were so that our fathers or the good man of the house had a mattress or flockbed and thereto a sack of chaff to rest his head upon, he thought himself to be well lodged as the lord of the town, that peradventure lay seldom in a bed of down or whole feathers. Pillows were thought meet only for women in childbed. As for servants, if they had any sheet above them, it was well, for seldom had they any under their bodies, to keep them from the pricking straws that ran oft through the canvas of the pallet and razed their hardened hides."

There had been many changes in lifestyle, and, subsequently, in accommodation since the battle at Bosworth, yet none of these were to compare to the effects, on all levels of society, that followed the Reformation.

The Dissolution of the Monasteries in 1538 marked Henry VIII's break with the Roman Church and the start of a more distinctive English culture. The word of the Bible now became the direct source of divine authority, rather than a priest's interpretation of the Bible, and literacy, the tool of commerce, began to flourish more than ever before. Power was wrested from the clerics - English agents acting on behalf of a foreign ruler, the Church of Rome - and transferred to practical laymen, in order to utilise the potentially vast capital of the Church directly for the benefit of the English empire.

Renaissance architecture tended towards the secular, following the anti-clerical revolution, for the prevailing opinion was that there were already enough churches. In fact, the monasteries and their lands were not so much dissolved as redistributed by the crown. Most of the land was sold, some was given to court favourites and the remainder was retained, to be sold as required in order to boost the crown's finances. The monastic buildings were converted to fulfil a variety of different uses, depending on the activities of the new owner, although some became homes, such as Lacock, Wiltshire (see page 18).

on the activities of the new owner, although some became homes, such as Lacock, Wiltshire (see page 18).

The reallocation of wealth and power away from the church and into the entrepreneurial sector formed the basis of huge personal fortunes that would create the great 'prodigy house' of the Elizabethan and Jacobite periods.

Development in Scotland was much slower than that in England until the Act of Union in 1707. Scottish central government was weaker during the 15th and 16th centuries, with the result that feudalism and the corresponding need for a defended home persisted much longer.

The Reformation took place in Scotland a generation later than in England, and the dissolution of the monasteries was organised less systematically than it had been under Henry VIII. Although Scotland had developed close links with Continental Europe, particularly France, as a result of the long-standing rivalry and wars with England, these relationships were primarily political, rather than cultural. As a result, few external artistic influences penetrated Scotland at that time, and although those that did were exploited to the utmost, the Scottish architects inevitably had to resort to recycling traditional themes.

By the late 16th century, Scotland was also experiencing the emergence of a new, more powerful class of landowner and merchant. However there were still no 'prodigy houses' or their equivalent, as the great Scottish families had neither the cultural outlook nor the convertible wealth of the English. They also lacked the inspiration of the absent Mary Queen of Scots.

Once the outer shell of defences became redundant, grand palaces and mansions began to flourish. The spread of literacy resulted in books becoming much more easily accessible, so that an architect or his patron no longer had to undertake a grand tour of Europe. The most popular and influential contemporary styles and ideas could be found on the pages of a book. The detail this presented found its way onto the drawing-board and, from there, to the elaborate and varied facades of Britain's historic stately homes.

Garry Gibbons, January 1994

LANHYDROCK HOUSE, CORNWALL
Built between 1630 and 1642, Lanhydrock is and always has been Cornwall's grandest
house. It was rebuilt following the original plan after being destroyed by fire in 1881.

Main photograph: MONTACUTE HOUSE, SOMERSET
The scale of the house indicates the status and influence enjoyed by Edward Phelips, Speaker of the House of Commons and Master of the Rolls, who commenced building at Montacute in the year of the Armada, 1588. The power of the Phelip family had diminished substantially by the middle of the 17th century, and this dip in the family fortunes was reflected in the changing role of the house, for it was only used as a quiet country retreat over the next 300 years.

Inset photograph: SHERBORNE CASTLE, DORSET
Having leased the old castle at Sherborne from Elizabeth I in 1592, Sir Walter Raleigh set about modernising the structure, but soon abandoned the attempt, deciding instead to build an entirely new home just to the south of the original site. The resulting 16th century mansion was home to Sir Walter for only a short time, as he was soon to fall from favour, ending his days on the scaffold in 1618. The year before his death, Sherborne Castle was granted to Sir John Digby, the English Ambassador to Spain, who carried out additions to the building in 1625. The park was landscaped by 'Capability' Brown in the 18th century.

WILTON HOUSE, WILTSHIRE
Phillip Herbert, Earl of Pembroke and Montgomery, Lord Chamberlain and close personal friend of Charles I, took possession of Wilton in the middle of the 17th century. The house is thought to have been based on a rough design sketched by Inigo Jones, which was passed to his associate, Isaac de Caux, to complete. Wilton was gutted by fire in 1647 and rebuilding started immediately. The interior was entirely the work of Inigo Jones and remains a tribute to his genius.

BOWOOD HOUSE, WILTSHIRE

The original house, dating from 1725 and designed by Sir Orlando Bridgeman, was demolished in the 1950s. The house which is there today began as additions to the original, built around two courtyards, including the stable and kitchens. In 1768, the first Marquess of Lansdowne commissioned Robert Adam to close off these two areas, creating the grand Orangery overlooking the park, which was landscaped by 'Capability' Brown.

Main photograph: CORSHAM COURT, WILTSHIRE
The history of Corsham can be traced back to the Saxon King of Wessex, Ethelred the Unready (978-1017), whose country palace and court was situated here. The present building was begun by Thomas Smythe in 1582 near the ruins of the old manor. The estate was eventually purchased by Paul Methuen in 1745, and it remains in this family today. The enlargement of the house and park was entrusted to 'Capability' Brown in 1760 and further additions were carried out by John Nash in 1800 under the instructions of Paul Cobb Methuen.

Inset photograph: STOURHEAD, WILTSHIRE
Built for Henry Hoare I in the early part of the 18th century, Stourhead was one of the first country houses in the Palladian style. Designed by Colen Campbell, Stourhead was completed in 1725, the year of Henry's death, and continued

LACOCK ABBEY, WILTSHIRE

Originally an Augustinian convent, founded in 1232, which continued to prosper until its dissolution in 1539.
The property was purchased by Sir William Sharrington, who converted the abbey into a house. By the 18th century, Lacock had passed into the Talbot family and the hall was rebuilt in the Gothic style by John Ivory Talbot.
In 1831 William Henry Fox Talbot produced the world's first photographic negative, showing a small oriel window in the south gallery.

LONGLEAT HOUSE, WILTSHIRE

The spot on which Longleat House stands is a reflection of the security which was brought to England by Henry VII. Scenically the position is perfect, but strategically it is virtually indefensible. The house was started by Sir John Thynne, who lavished a great deal of time and money on it from 1547 until his death in 1580, and although the great Elizabethan architect, Robert Smythson, worked on the project, Longleat is unquestionably the work of Sir John. This magnificent home, and England's first Renaissance house, remains home to the Thynne family, Marquesses of Bath.

Main and inset picture: BEAULIEU, HAMPSHIRE
The Palace House of Beaulieu was developed around the original gate house to the great Cistercian abbey founded by King John. The house owes its present appearance to work carried out by the architect, Sir Arthur Bloomfield, in 1872. Beaulieu passed to the Montague family following the Dissolution of the Monasteries in 1538, and is still home to the Montagues today.

Main photograph: PETWORTH HOUSE, WEST SUSSEX
Built around an early 14th century house, which still remains at its core, Petworth was constructed in French Baroque style by the sixth Duke of Somerset in 1688-93. In 1714 a fire destroyed the dome which sat above the central three bays, along with hipped-roofs that crowned the three bay projections at each end.

Inset photograph: IGHTHAM MOTE, KENT
The earliest part of this manor house dates from the 1340s, and although it has been subject to continual development over the past 600 years, it has lost little of its medieval character. The first recorded owner was Sir Thomas Cawne, a soldier from Staffordshire who fought with the Black Knight at Crecy and went on to marry a Kentish woman. The Cawnes maintained their ownership of Ightham until the 15th century, when the house changed hands many times.

Main and inset picture: BROADLANDS, HAMPSHIRE
A small Tudor manor stood on this spot when, in 1736, William Kent was commissioned by the first Viscount Palmerston to deflect the course of the River Test through its gardens. About thirty years later 'Capability' Brown landscaped the park and, under the second Viscount, set about transforming the manor into a fine Palladian house. Brown's son-in-law, Henry Holland, completed his work.

BLENHEIM PALACE, OXFORDSHIRE

A national monument to the services of John Churchill, first Duke of Marlborough and hero of the Battle of Blenheim, which put an end to Louis XIV's hopes of European domination. Plans for the palace were drawn up by John Vanbrugh, a successful playwright who had turned architect five years earlier. Vanbrugh was one of the greatest exponents of the Baroque style. The Marlboroughs were to fall from favour in 1710 and the work was completed at the Duke's own expense in 1716. The Duchess forced Vanbrugh to resign the commission after her "intolerable treatment" of him, for the Duchess, on her own admission, "mortally hated all gardens and architecture". The park and lake were the creations of the ubiquitous 'Capability' Brown.

OWLPEN MANOR, GLOUCESTERSHIRE

One of the most picturesque medieval manor houses in the country. Owlpen was the home of Marjery Ollepen in the 16th century, and her marriage to John Daunt heralded the start of many alterations and additions, particularly the hall and Great Chamber above it. This work was completed around 1540. The west wing was added by Thomas Daunt in 1616, and the east wing dates from 1720.

Main and inset photographs: BUCKINGHAM PALACE, LONDON
The original home of the Duke of Buckingham bears little resemblance to the grand palace on this site today.
The original palace was built in 1705 by the architect William Winde, and King George III and Queen Charlotte
moved there in 1762. Their son, George IV, considered it too small, and commissioned John Nash to provide
something more spacious and luxurious. Building work continued for two years until, in 1828, the expenditure
became a national scandal. After the death of George IV in 1830, Nash was dismissed, his career finished.
Queen Victoria later commissioned Edward Blore to enlarge the palace by adding a fourth wing, which is now the
front face. The Nash facade can only be seen from the palace gardens (see inset).

CHISWICK HOUSE, GREATER LONDON
Designed in 1724 by the third Earl of Burlington, Chiswick House was the one of the first examples of the
increasing trend towards classicism in the architectural design of this era. Built as an annexe to an earlier house,
now demolished, this Italian-style villa stands as an expression of Burlington's personal vision of antiquity.

Main and inset photograph: HAMPTON COURT PALACE, GREATER LONDON
Cardinal Thomas Wolsey, Archbishop of York and Lord Chancellor of England, bought the
manor of Hampton after asking an international panel of doctors to advise him on the healthiest
place within twenty miles of London. The seat he built comprised about 1000 rooms, the con-
tents of which included 280 silken beds which were kept at the ready for visitors. A Venetian
ambassador reported, "To reach his audience chamber one must pass through eight rooms; all are
hung with tapestry, which is changed once a week". The cardinal became the victim of Henry
VIII's fury during the King's battle to divorce Catherine of Aragon, so Wolsey presented Henry
with Hampton in an effort to placate him. Extensive rebuilding work was carried out by Henry
and his second wife, Anne Boleyn. Following Henry's death, Hampton Court continued as a royal
palace much as he left it, until William and Mary commissioned Sir Christopher Wren to set
about a major programme of alterations and rebuilding.

Main and inset photographs: SYON HOUSE, GREATER LONDON
A monastery founded by Henry V originally stood on this site until the property fell to the crown after the Dissolution of Monasteries Act of 1539. The Duke of Somerset, 'Protector of the Realm', appropriated the land following the succession of the nine year old Edward VI. The Duke began construction of the house, but, soon after its completion, he was charged with felony and executed. The house was subsequently associated with a series of similar tragedies. Lady Jane Grey was offered the crown at Syon, only to reign for just nine days before going to the block. Elizabeth I granted the house to Henry Percy, ninth Earl of Northumberland, who was falsely implicated in the Gunpowder Plot. The house was to serve as prison to the children of Charles I following the Civil War. Syon eventually passed to the first Duke of Northumberland, who engaged 'Capability' Brown to landscape the grounds, and Robert Adam to transform the house. The Great Conservatory was designed by Charles Fowler, who went on to build the Covent Garden Market.

Main photograph: ROUSHAM PARK HOUSE, OXFORDSHIRE
Built in 1635 by Sir Robert Dormer, Rousham remains home to the Dormer family. The house was remodelled in 1738-40 by William Kent, but it was his work on the gardens that really distinguished Rousham from other, similar houses.

Inset photograph: FIFIELD MANOR, OXFORDSHIRE
A stone manor dating from circa 1320, the medieval great hall is concealed by the Elizabethan facade.

WOBURN ABBEY, BEDFORDSHIRE

The old abbey was left to John Russel, first Earl of Bedford, in the will of Henry VIII. Over the next seventy-five years the abbey lay uninhabited, falling into ruin, until, in 1625, a plague swept through London. The fourth Earl, Francis Russel, fled the capital and escaped to Woburn. Two years later he commissioned Isaac de Caux to build him a house, of which only one wing is still standing, as over the course of the next hundred years Woburn suffered from neglect. The third Duke gambled away a fortune and died in 1732 at the age of twenty-four. The fourth Duke eventually restored the family finances sufficiently to start rebuilding work in 1747. Further work was carried out by Henry Holland under the instructions of the fifth Duke.

FROGMORE HOUSE, BERKSHIRE
Built in the 17th century, Frogmore is one of the least known royal residences, situated within the private home park at Windsor Castle. It was a favourite residence of Queen Charlotte and also of the Duchess of Kent, Queen Victoria's mother.

Main and inset photographs: SANDRINGHAM, NORFOLK

Sandringham was built on the site of an earlier property in the second half of the 18th century by Cornish Henley, who died before its completion. His son sold it to a neighbour, who, on his death in 1843, left it to his friend, Charles Spenser Cowper. The house was then purchased by Queen Victoria in 1862 for her son, the future Edward VII, as a holiday home. Sandringham was remodelled and enlarged as Edward's family and household grew in numbers. The house is still one of the residences of the Royal family.

CASTLE HOWARD, YORKSHIRE

Seat of the Howard family, Castle Howard was John Vanbrugh's first work. Built for the first Earl of Carlisle, the house was eventually completed in 1750 by Sir Thomas Robinson, Lord Carlisle's son-in-law. The house displays the difference between Vanbrugh's Baroque and Robinson's Palladian styles.

CHATSWORTH, DERBYSHIRE

One of the great houses of England, home to the Dukes of Devonshire. The first house on this site dates from 1551, three years after Sir William Cavendish and his wife, Bess of Hardwick, bought the land. Reconstruction of the house took place under the first Duke from 1686, whilst 'Capability' Brown landscaped the park in the 18th century. Chatsworth grew to its present stature as a result of the remodelling carried out by Sir Jeffrey Wyatville in the early 19th century.

HAREWOOD HOUSE, WEST YORKSHIRE

The estate was bought by Henry Lascelles in 1738, after he had made his fortune in sugar plantations. His son Edwin, first Lord of Harewood, landscaped the park with the assistance of 'Capability' Brown and had the house built to the designs of John Carr and Robert Adam. Harewood House was later remodelled by Charles Barry for the third Earl of Harewood in 1843.

SIZERGH CASTLE, CUMBRIA

Ancient seat of the Stricklands, Sizergh was built around a pele tower dating from about 1340 with the addition of a Great Hall in the 15th century. A new Elizabethan block and wings were completed later, and further remodelling was undertaken around 1770, to the designs of John Hird of Cartmel.

Main photograph: HOLKER HALL, CUMBRIA

Holker is a Victorian country home, which was built on the site of a 17th century house. The house is the result of two building phases undertaken for the seventh Duke of Devonshire. One wing was put up by George Webster in 1840 and, following a fire, the other was raised by Paley and Austin in 1873.

Inset photograph: HUTTON-IN-THE-FOREST, CUMBRIA

A conglomerate of various styles and dates around a central 14th century pele tower. In 1606 the estate was bought from Lancelot Hutton by a rich merchant, Richard Fletcher of Cockermouth. His son, Sir Henry Fletcher, first Baronet, added the long gallery in 1641-5 to the design of the 'excellent skillful mason and carver', Alexander Pogmire.

WALLINGTON HALL, NORTHUMBERLAND
Built in 1688 by Sir William Blackett, the present Georgian house was remodelled for Walter Calverly who lived at
Wallington from 1728 to 1777. Following Walter's death the house passed to his nephew, Sir John Trevelyan, whose fam-

CRAGSIDE, NORTHUMBERLAND
Built up over a fifteen year period, Cragside is the creation of the first Lord Armstrong, inventor, engineer and arms man-

WALES

Main photograph: BRYN BRAS, GWYNEDD
Built in the Romanesque style and dating from 1830, this sham castle is constructed around an early farm house whose walls form the core of the present building.

Inset photograph: PENRHYN CASTLE, GWYNEDD
Commissioned by Lord Penrhyn, building work began under the direction of Thomas Hopper in 1820 and continued for 17 years. Penrhyn Castle is a particularly fine example of the Norman Revival style and is regarded as the architect's masterpiece. Its opulence reflects the wealth acquired through the Penrhyn slate quarries.

PLAS NEWYDD, ISLE OF ANGLESEY, GWYNEDD
Home to the Marquess of Anglesey, this 18th century Georgian style mansion is situated beside the Menai Strait, with spectacular views of Snowdonia.

PLAS NEWYDD, CLWYD

The history of this extraordinary house is closely linked to that of its extraordinary owners. The black and white timbered building was created around an old farmhouse by the so-called 'Ladies of Llangollen' - Lady Eleanor Butler, the Honourable Sarah Ponsonby and their maid, Mary 'Molly the Basher' Carryll - who moved there in 1780 in order to escape the restrictive formalities of Irish country life. Their visitors included Wellington, Wordsworth, Shelley and Byron.

Main photograph: TRETOWER COURT, POWYS
Tretower Court was extensively developed by Sir Roger Vaughan following the move, in the 14th century, from the fortified keep that still stands close by. A notable stone and timber-framed medieval house, Tretower comprises two wings either side of a courtyard and a large gate house at the entrance.

Inset photograph: ERDDIG, CLWYD
A late 17th century house built by Joshua Edisbury, Erddig was later refurbished by John Mellor, a wealthy London lawyer, who bought the property in 1716. It then passed to his nephew, Simon Yorke, and remained in his family until 1973.

Main photograph: LAMPHEY BISHOP'S PALACE, DYFED
Lamphey Palace is thought to have been a retreat of the Welsh bishops of St David's before the Norman occupation.
By 1326 the sole occupant of this comfortable and picturesque palace was Bishop David Martin. However, it was
Bishop William Gower, builder of St David's Palace, who elevated Lamphey to its heights of splendour.

Inset photograph: ST DAVID'S BISHOPS PALACE, DYFED
Although ruined, St David's is still recognisable as a magnificent building. Three imposing wings surround a courtyard with the chief apartments built at the first floor level. The Great Hall was added by Bishop Henry de Gower in
the early 14th century.

TREDEGAR HOUSE, GWENT
Ancestral home to the Lords of Tredegar, this superior Renaissance house was largely rebuilt around an open court by Sir William Morgan in about 1670. The house stands in extensive parkland and boasts a fine restoration facade.

SCOTLAND

DUNROBIN CASTLE, HIGHLANDS
Home to the Dukes of Sutherland, this large palace in the Franco-Scottish style was designed by Sir Charles Barry during the period 1835-1850. Dunrobin replaced an original 13th century stronghold, whose massive square keep

Main photograph: BALMORAL, GRAMPIAN

Although Balmoral will forever be linked with the memory of Queen Victoria, the estate dates from the late 15th century and the Abergeldie Gordon family. In the 17th century ownership passed to the Farquhasons and from them to the Earls of Fife. The Gordons returned to the estate when Sir Robert Gordon took possession and the castle's appearance today owes much to the reconstruction work carried out by him. Queen Victoria heard of Balmoral following a visit there by her physician's son. The enthusiastic reports about the climate and scenery led Queen Victoria to buy the lease, sight unseen, following Sir Robert's death. The Queen wrote of her new holiday home "the scenery all around is the finest almost I have seen anywhere...we are certainly in the finest part of the Highlands and quite in the heart of them...".

Inset photograph: LEITH HALL, LOTHIAN

A mansion house dating from the 1650's, with new wings added in the 18th and 19th centuries.

Main photograph: FALKLAND PALACE, FIFE
Falkland passed to the Stuarts in 1370 and quickly became a favourite hunting location. James IV built a new palace in
Scottish Gothic style, although the alterations which James V made between 1537 and 1542 are entirely different.
Following a visit to the French court, James was inspired by the French Renaissance style.

Inset photograph: SCONE PALACE, TAYSIDE
Home to the first recorded Parliaments and the famous Stone of Scone, upon which the Scottish kings were crowned, this
is the historic heart of Scotland. The present house was designed by William Atkinson for the third Earl of Mansfield.

LINLITHGOW PALACE, LOTHIAN

Birthplace of Mary Queen of Scots in 1542, Linlithgow Palace has retained some of its former splendour, despite the effect of two major fires during its 600 year history. Once a fine royal residence, the palace grew round a quadrangle and tower built by Edward of England, though much of this was destroyed by the first fire in 1424. Over the next 300 years its grandeur and prominence was rebuilt, only to suffer the ravages of fire again in 1746.

Main and inset photograph: PALACE OF HOLYROODHOUSE, LOTHIAN

An Augustinian abbey was founded here by David I in 1128 and, as the abbey was of royal foundation, the founder and his successors would have been frequent guests. This made the abbey (see inset) a natural target for attack during the many long wars with England. The abbey became a royal favourite from the 15th century when James I chose Holyrood as the birthplace for his son, who was later crowned James II there. The great quadrangular palace which exists today dates from the 16th century. James IV rebuilt that part of the abbey used as a royal residence around three sides of an open square, which was surrounded by an outer court. This late medieval palace was completed by James V who added a tower and fourth range, enclosing the open side of the square. Following years of strife and neglect, Holyroodhouse was extensively rebuilt by Charles II. The range built by James V was retained and a further tower was added to balance the

HOPETOUN HOUSE, LOTHIAN
A fine mansion, seat of the Earls of Hopetoun and, later, the Marquesses of Linlithgow. Enlarged by William Adam and his son, John, from 1721-1754, Hopetoun is one of Scotland's great houses and remains home to the Hope family.

Main photograph: DALMENY HOUSE, LOTHIAN
Scotland's first Gothic Revival house, Dalmeny was built by William Wilkins in 1815 for the fourth Earl of Rosebery. The Earl's previous home, nearby Barnbougle Castle, stood on the shore of the Firth of Clyde and was much neglected - the third Earl was once drenched by a large wave that came through the dining-room window.

Inset photograph: GOSFORD HOUSE, LOTHIAN
The Wemyss-Charteris family acquired the Gosford Estate in 1781 and, working to the designs of Robert Adam, building soon began on the present house. Although well established at their home in Amisfield, the family felt that the golfing was better in the Gosford area.

LENNOXLOVE, LOTHIAN
Built around a mid 14th century tower house, Lennoxlove was extensively remodelled by the Duke of

THIRLESTANE CASTLE, BORDERS
Rebuilt in the 16th century on the site of an earlier 13th century fort, Thirlestane has been enlarged and embellished over the centuries. It is the seat of the Duke of Lauderdale.

Main photograph: FLOORS CASTLE, BORDERS
Described as Scotland's largest occupied building, Floors Castle was built by William Adam between the years 1721-1725.
Ancestral home to the Dukes of Roxburghe, Floors owes much of its present appearance to the additions carried out by
William Playfair in the 1830s.

Inset photograph: MALLERSTAIN, BORDERS
Home to the Earl and Countess Haddington, Mallerstain was begun in 1725 by William Adam and completed several
years later by his son, Robert. A grand Georgian mansion, the Italian style gardens were laid out by Sir Reginald
Blomfield.

DRUMLANRIG CASTLE, DUMFRIES & GALLOWAY
The 17th century Dumfriesshire home to the Dukes of Buccleuch and Queensberry. Built on the site of the orig-
inal 14th century Douglas stronghold, Drumlanrig was probably designed by the King's Master Mason, Robert
Mylne, for the 1st Duke, William Douglas from 1679-1691.

HISTORIC HOUSES
OF BRITAIN

75

77

77

79

79

81 86 83 86
81 88
GLASGOW EDINBURGH
90 92
92
94
60
58
NEWCASTLE

56

54
56
48
52
LEEDS
MANCHESTER
50
64 62
62
68
66

46

BIRMINGHAM

70
40 40 42
68 28
70
SWANSEA 30
72 32
16 14 44 38 34
CARDIFF 18 36 LONDON
BRISTOL
20 24
16 12
10 10 26
24
22

8

© The Automobile Association 1994